Jack Kent's

TWELVE DAYS of CHRISTMAS

PARENTS' MAGAZINE PRESS · NEW YORK

Twelve days of Christmas (English folk song)
  Jack Kent's Twelve days of Christmas.
    SUMMARY: *A young girl's joy turns to dismay as*
larger and larger gifts arrive from her true love each
day of the Christmas season.
    1. Folk-songs, English.   2. Christmas music
[1. Folk songs, English.   2. Christmas music]
I.   Kent, Jack, 1920-   illus. II.   Title.
PZ8.3T8517Ke   [E]   73-1823
ISBN 0-8193-0696-7
ISBN 0-8193-0697-5 (lib. bdg.)

On the first day of Christmas
my true love gave to me
a partridge in a pear tree.

On the second day of Christmas
my true love gave to me
two turtledoves and
a partridge in a pear tree.

On the third day of Christmas
my true love gave to me
three French hens, two turtledoves,
and a partridge in a pear tree.

On the fourth day of Christmas my true love gave to me four collie birds, three French hens, two turtledoves, and a partridge in a pear tree.

On the fifth day of Christmas my true love gave to me five golden rings, four collie birds, three French hens, two turtledoves, and a partridge in a pear tree.

On the sixth day of Christmas my true love gave to me six geese
a-laying, five golden rings, four collie birds, three French hens,
two turtledoves, and a partridge in a pear tree.

On the seventh day
of Christmas
my true love gave to me
seven swans a-swimming
six geese a-laying,
five golden rings,
four collie birds,
three French hens,.
two turtledoves,
and a partridge
in a pear tree.

On the eighth day of Christmas my true love gave to me eight maids a-milking, seven swans a-swimming, six geese a-laying, five golden rings, four collie birds, three French hens, two turtledoves, and a partridge in a pear tree.

On the ninth day of Christmas my true love gave to me nine pipers piping, eight maids a-milking, seven swans a-swimming, six geese a-laying, five golden rings, four collie birds, three French hens, two turtledoves, and a partridge in a pear tree.

On the tenth day of Christmas my true love
gave to me ten drummers drumming,
nine pipers piping, eight maids a-milking,
seven swans a-swimming, six geese a-laying,
five golden rings, four collie birds,
three French hens, two turtledoves,
and a partridge in a pear tree.

On the eleventh day of Christmas
my true love gave to me eleven lords
a-leaping, ten drummers drumming,
nine pipers piping, eight maids
a-milking, seven swans a-swimming,
six geese a-laying, five golden rings,
four collie birds, three French hens,
two turtledoves, and a partridge
in a pear tree.

On the twelfth day of Christmas my true love gave to me twelve ladies
dancing, eleven lords a-leaping, ten drummers drumming, nine pipers piping,

eight maids a-milking, seven swans a-swimming, six geese a-laying, five golden rings, four collie birds, three French hens, two turtledoves...

... and a partridge in a pear tree.